$19.95

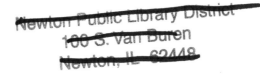

PRO SPORTS
SUPERSTARS

Superstars
of the
PHILADELPHIA PHILLIES

by Annabelle Tometich

amicus
high interest

Amicus High Interest is published by Amicus
P.O. Box 1329, Mankato, MN 56002
www.amicuspublishing.us

Library of Congress Cataloging-in-Publication Data
Tometich, Annabelle, 1980-
   Superstars of the Philadelphia Phillies / by Annabelle Tometich.
      pages cm. -- (Pro sports superstars)
   Includes index.
   Summary: "Presents some of the Philadelphia Phillies' greatest players
and their achievements in pro baseball, including Jimmy Rollins, Chase
Utley, and Ryan Howard"--Provided by publisher.
   ISBN 978-1-60753-595-9 (hardcover) -- ISBN 978-1-60753-629-1 (pdf
ebook)
   1. Philadelphia Phillies (Baseball team)--History--Juvenile literature. I.
Title.
   GV875.P45T65 2014
   796.357'640974811--dc23
                                   2013044094

Photo Credits: Jeff Robeson/AP Images, cover; Photo Works/Shutterstock
Images, 2, 18; Matt Slocum/AP Images, 5; Library of Congress, 6;
Bettmann/Corbis, 8, 11, 12; Jacques M. Chenet/Corbis, 15; J Pat Carter/AP
Images, 16, 22; Al Behrman/AP Images, 21

Produced for Amicus by The Peterson Publishing Company
and Red Line Editorial.

Editor Arnold Ringstad
Designer Maggie Villaume
Printed in the United States of America
Mankato, MN
2-2014
PA10001
10 9 8 7 6 5 4 3 2 1

TABLE OF CONTENTS

MEET THE PHILADELPHIA PHILLIES

The Philadelphia Phillies are more than 130 years old. They have won two **World Series** titles. The Phillies have had many stars. Here are some of the best.

6

GROVER CLEVELAND ALEXANDER

Grover Cleveland Alexander was a great pitcher. He won many games. In 1915 he led the Phillies to their first **National League** title.

Alexander was named after a US president. Friends called him Pete.

ROBIN ROBERTS

Robin Roberts threw very hard pitches. He started playing in 1948. Roberts struck out 2,357 batters in his career.

RICHIE ASHBURN

Richie Ashburn was a great hitter. He played center field. Ashburn was quick on his feet. He made many great catches. He played in six **All-Star Games**. The first was in 1948.

The 1950 team was called The Whiz Kids. Many players were young.

11

STEVE CARLTON

Steve Carlton was a pitcher.
He struck out more than 4,000
batters in his career. He helped
the Phillies win the World Series
in 1980.

MIKE SCHMIDT

Mike Schmidt was a great third baseman. He won 10 **Gold Glove Awards**. Schmidt also hit with great power. He played his whole career for the Phillies.

In 1976 Schmidt hit four home runs in one game.

JIMMY ROLLINS

Jimmy Rollins is a great **shortstop**.

In 2007 he won an **MVP** award.

Rollins is quick on his feet. He

helped the Phillies win the 2008

World Series.

CHASE UTLEY

Chase Utley plays second base.

His swing is smooth and powerful.

Utley has played in five All-Star

Games. The first was in 2006.

Utley hit a grand slam in his first game with the Phillies.

RYAN HOWARD

Ryan Howard plays first base. He is tall and strong. In 2006 Howard hit 58 home runs. He won an MVP Award that year.

The Phillies have had many great superstars. Who will be next?

TEAM FAST FACTS

Founded: 1883

Nicknames: The Phils, the Fightin' Phils, the Phightin' Phils

Home Stadium: Citizens Bank Park (Philadelphia, Pennsylvania)

World Series Championships: 2 (1980, 2008)

Hall of Fame Players: 32, including Grover Cleveland Alexander, Richie Ashburn, Robin Roberts, Mike Schmidt, and Steve Carlton

WORDS TO KNOW

All-Star Game – a game between the best players in baseball each year

Gold Glove Awards – awards given to the best fielders each year

grand slam – a home run hit when all three bases have runners on them, scoring four runs

home runs – hits that go far enough to leave the field, letting the hitter run all the way around the bases to score a run

MVP – Most Valuable Player; an honor given to the best player each season

National League – one of two leagues in Major League baseball. It has 15 teams.

shortstop – a player whose main job is to stop balls hit between second and third base

World Series – the annual baseball championship series

LEARN MORE

Books

Gilbert, Sara. *World Series Champs: Philadelphia Phillies*. Mankato, MN: Creative Education, 2013.

Kelley, K. C. *Philadelphia Phillies (Favorite Baseball Teams)*. North Mankato, MN: The Child's World, 2013.

Web Sites

Baseball History
http://mlb.mlb.com/mlb/history
Learn more about the history of baseball.

MLB.com
http://mlb.com
See pictures and track your favorite baseball player's stats.

Philadelphia Phillies – Official Site
http://philadelphia.phillies.mlb.com
Watch video clips and read stories about the Philadelphia Phillies.

INDEX